W9-ATT-649

GEOTHERMAL ENERGY

PUTTING EARTH'S HEAT TO WORK

JESSIE ALKIRE

Consulting Editor, Diane Craig, M.A./Reading Specialist

Super Sandcastle

An Imprint of Abdo Publishing
abdopublishing.com

abdopublishing.com

Published by Abdo Publishing, a division of ABDO, PO Box 398166, Minneapolis, Minnesota 55439. Copyright © 2019 by Abdo Consulting Group, Inc. International copyrights reserved in all countries. No part of this book may be reproduced in any form without written permission from the publisher. Super SandCastle™ is a trademark and logo of Abdo Publishing.

Printed in the United States of America, North Mankato, Minnesota

052018
092018

THIS BOOK CONTAINS
RECYCLED MATERIALS

Design and Production: Mighty Media, Inc.
Editor: Megan Borgert-Spaniol
Cover Photographs: Getty Images; Shutterstock
Interior Photographs: Getty Images; iStockphoto; Mighty Media, Inc.; Shutterstock; Wikimedia Commons

Library of Congress Control Number: 2017961849

Publisher's Cataloging-in-Publication Data
Names: Alkire, Jessie, author.
Title: Geothermal energy: Putting Earth's heat to work / by Jessie Alkire.
Other titles: Putting Earth's heat to work
Description: Minneapolis, Minnesota : Abdo Publishing, 2019. | Series: Earth's
    energy innovations
Identifiers: ISBN 9781532115714 (lib.bdg.) | ISBN 9781532156434 (ebook)
Subjects: LCSH: Geothermal resources--Juvenile literature. | Power resources--
    Juvenile literature. | Energy development--Juvenile literature. | Energy
    conversion--Juvenile literature.
Classification: DDC 621.44--dc23

Super SandCastle™ books are created by a team of professional educators, reading specialists, and content developers around five essential components—phonemic awareness, phonics, vocabulary, text comprehension, and fluency—to assist young readers as they develop reading skills and strategies and increase their general knowledge. All books are written, reviewed, and leveled for guided reading, early reading intervention, and Accelerated Reader™ programs for use in shared, guided, and independent reading and writing activities to support a balanced approach to literacy instruction.

CONTENTS

What Is Geothermal Energy?   4

Energy Timeline   6

Hot Springs   8

Geothermal Power   10

Growing Resource   12

Electricity and Heat   14

Power Plants   16

Heat Pumps   18

Heating Up   20

More About Geothermal Energy   22

Test Your Knowledge   23

Glossary   24

WHAT IS GEOTHERMAL ENERGY?

Geothermal energy is the energy of Earth's heat. The inside of Earth is very hot. It **contains** liquid rock called magma. Magma heats underground rocks and water. This produces hot water and steam.

Hot water and steam collect in underground **reservoirs**. Humans capture energy from the reservoirs. It is used to produce heat and power!

Magma at Earth's surface is called lava.

Geothermal energy is renewable. This is because Earth is always producing heat.

ENERGY TIMELINE

8000s BCE

Native Americans use **hot springs** for cooking.

1892 CE

The first **district heating system** is created in Boise, Idaho.

1904

Piero Ginori Conti uses geothermal steam to light five light bulbs.

Discover how geothermal energy has changed over time!

1913

The first geothermal power plant opens in Larderello, Italy.

1960

The first large US geothermal power plant opens in California.

2016

Less than 1 percent of US electricity comes from geothermal energy.

HOT SPRINGS

Ancient Roman bath fed by hot spring water

Hot springs are sources of geothermal energy. Native Americans used them for cooking around 8000 BCE. Ancient Greeks and Romans bathed in hot springs.

The first geothermal **district heating system** was created in 1892. It was in Boise, Idaho. Water from hot springs was piped into buildings. This provided heat!

Hot springs are thought to have healing effects on humans who swim in them.

GEOTHERMAL POWER

Piero Ginori Conti produced geothermal electricity in 1904. He used natural steam in Larderello, Italy. The first geothermal power plant opened there in 1913.

The first large US geothermal plant opened in 1960. It was in California. More power plants opened over time.

Larderello power plant

PIERO GINORI CONTI

BORN: June 3, 1865, Florence, Italy

DIED: December 3, 1939, Florence, Italy

Piero Ginori Conti was an Italian businessman. He experimented with natural steam in Larderello, Italy. In 1904, Conti used steam to light five light bulbs. In 1913, the first geothermal power plant opened in Larderello. It still operates today!

GROWING RESOURCE

Mayon volcano in the Philippines

Many countries use geothermal energy today. Much of the power produced in Iceland and the Philippines is geothermal. Earth's heat escapes through **volcanoes** and **hot springs** in these countries.

The United States is the leading producer of geothermal power. But geothermal is still a growing energy **resource**. In 2016, less than 1 percent of US electricity came from geothermal energy.

Most US geothermal plants are in western states. Hot water and steam reservoirs are common there.

ELECTRICITY AND HEAT

Geothermal power plant

Geothermal energy is used to produce electricity. Geothermal power plants are all over the world. They are common where magma rises near Earth's surface. These areas often have **hot springs**, **geysers**, or **volcanoes**.

Geothermal energy is also used for heating. Hot springs provide direct heat. And heat pumps draw geothermal energy from underground. This heats buildings and other structures.

Iceland's famous Strokkur geyser erupts every few minutes.

POWER PLANTS

Some geothermal power plants use natural steam from **reservoirs**. Others pump hot water from underground. The water turns into steam at the surface.

The steam energy turns a **turbine**. The turbine rotates a **generator**. This creates electricity. The electricity powers homes and businesses!

Steam turbine

Steam used in power plants is cooled back into water. The water is pumped underground to be heated again!

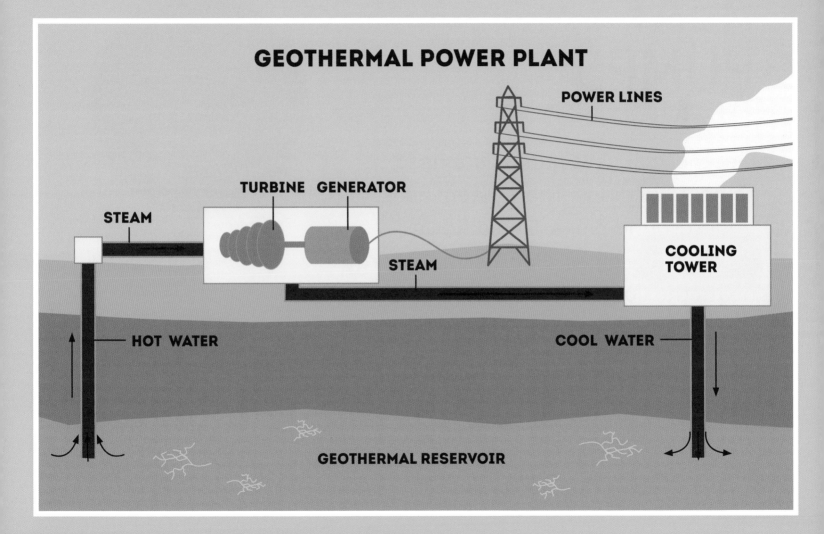

GEOTHERMAL POWER PLANT

POWER LINES

TURBINE   GENERATOR

STEAM

STEAM

COOLING TOWER

HOT WATER

COOL WATER

GEOTHERMAL RESERVOIR

HEAT PUMPS

Geothermal heat pumps are used to heat buildings. This system uses underground pipes. Liquid flows through the pipes. Geothermal energy heats the liquid. The liquid is pumped to the surface. This heats the building.

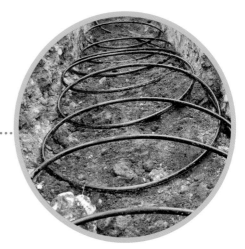

Piping for geothermal heat pump

This system also cools buildings during summer. Surface air heats the liquid. Then underground pipes **absorb** this heat. The cooled liquid is pumped back to the surface. This cools the building!

*Heat pumps work because the temperature underground is constant.
It is warmer than the air in winter. And it's cooler than the air in summer.*

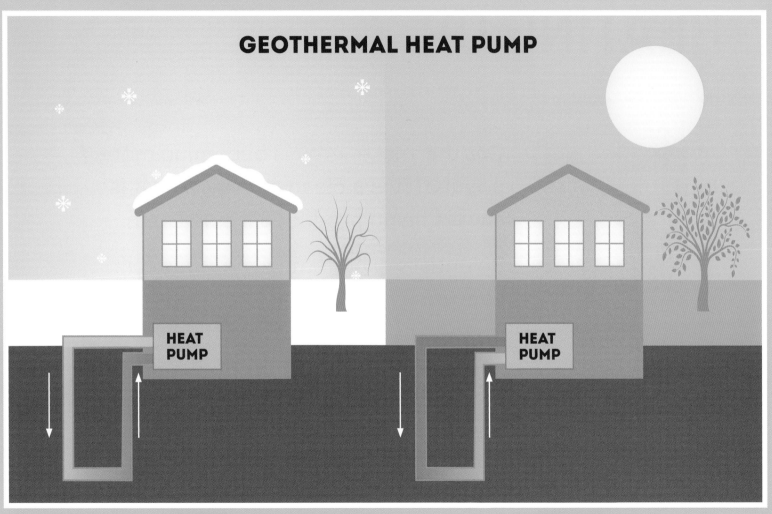

GEOTHERMAL HEAT PUMP

HEAT PUMP

HEAT PUMP

WINTER

SUMMER

HEATING UP

Geothermal energy is becoming more popular. It is a clean energy. And it is always being produced inside Earth.

Scientists explore new methods for capturing geothermal energy. One method pumps water into the ground. The water hits hot rock and turns into steam. Methods like this could help power the **future**!

People drill into Earth to capture geothermal energy.

The Geysers is a group of geothermal power plants in California. It is the world's largest producer of geothermal power.

MORE ABOUT GEOTHERMAL ENERGY

Do you want to tell others about geothermal energy? Here are some fun facts to share!

MORE THAN HALF OF ICELAND'S HOMES are heated by geothermal energy.

MANY GEOTHERMAL SOURCES are in the Pacific Ring of Fire. This region is known for its many **volcanoes**.

CALIFORNIA produces 72 percent of US geothermal electricity.

TEST YOUR KNOWLEDGE

1. Where was the first US **district heating system**?

2. In what year did Piero Ginori Conti first produce geothermal electricity?

3. Geothermal energy can also be used for cooling. **TRUE OR FALSE?**

THINK ABOUT IT!

Have you ever seen a **geyser** erupt? This is geothermal energy at work!

ANSWERS: 1. Boise, Idaho 2. 1904 3. True

GLOSSARY

absorb – to soak up or take in.

contain – to consist of or include.

district heating system – a system of pipes that delivers heat from a central location to many users.

future – the time that hasn't happened yet.

generator – a machine that creates electricity.

geyser – a hot spring that shoots out hot water and steam.

hot spring – a natural flow of heated water from underground.

reservoir – a natural or human-made place where something is stored.

resource – something that is usable or valuable.

turbine – a machine that produces power when it is rotated at high speed.

volcano – a deep opening in Earth's surface from which hot liquid rock or steam comes out.